MW01222731

The Odd Puppet Odyssey

AN ADULT EPIC ON A SMALL STAGE

The Odd Puppet Odyssey

An Adult Epic on a Small Stage

Poetry by
RICHARD GOLD

Illustrations by
CELESTE ERICSSON

Mark & Angela,
Thanks for visiting
Pongo at Bumbershoot
Hope you enjoy these
adventures —

Richard Gold
9/1/13

BLACK HERON PRESS
Seattle, WA

Published in 2003, by

BLACK HERON PRESS
Post Office Box 95676
Seattle, WA 98145
www.blackheronpress.com

ISBN 0-930773-68-3

For Perry

CONTENTS

ILLUSTRATIONS

THE ODD PUPPET ODYSSEY

MERRILY, MERRILY, AN ODD PUPPET ODYSSEY

At the start
of these adventures,
Pongo and Rico, a modest pair of magical puppets,
are up a ladder for Geppetto in red wool sweaters
pulling leaves out of the gutters
and throwing them to the ground in
black, soggy clumps,
getting ready for a dead season,
with old candy stuck inside their pockets,

when they notice a noisy bird overhead,
the ugly duckling's panicky mother,
neck extended, scattering feathers,
squawking at the two broad-shouldered lady cops
and the convenience store manager
who chase her darling up and down
the median strip of the freeway.

The ugly duckling feels like poison,
accused, as he is,

of leaving a small green smear in front of the Slurpee machine
next to a man in broken shoes
with smashed backs and untied laces. The
duckling was standing there tired and indecisive,
and the man was swallowing half of a hot dog
and reaching for a glazed doughnut,
when something happened.

Yet only this morning Ugly was by the lake
in a rare and awkward good mood,
charging around the playground equipment,
quacking strange bugle calls under his breath,
unintentionally scattering smaller children
in their hats with flaps.
He was happy because last night
Geppetto bedded him down
with the Cowboy and Indian puppets
in a carefully marked box.

But Ugly soon felt
that his gunslinging compadres wanted him gone
because of his passivity and because of his efforts
to impress and mollify the Sheriff

who wore an expensive black sweater with a large diamond pattern.
Ugly achingly worried
that it was
his poor defense
that cost the team its young phenom, Tino,
a crack shot with a beautiful smile.

Then the smear incident,

and the ugly duckling was understandably self-conscious
at the day's wrap-up meeting,
walking slowly across the community room and
swinging his butt in a wide arc
onto the sagging couch, feeling emotional.

And Pongo and Rico, sensitive to the facts,
had to ask themselves if there was something malicious
in Geppetto's sorting, generally.
They remembered the pumpkin that rotted before Halloween
and how G encouraged it to run for
president of the Freshman class.
And how G stored the sexually active puppets
in a tin box.

Then there was the way he took the royal puppet
from *The Princess and the Pea* and cast her
as Blanche DuBois
opposite Mr. Punchinello.
And for colleagues he gave D'Artagnan
a drunk, an insecure womanizer, and a narcissistic architect
to hang out with in the bar at the Paris Hyatt.
Over time, the princess seemed less and less
like a giggling sunrise,
and D'Artagnan's flashing swordplay
never lived up to expectations.

Or were the puppets expecting too much
out of their associations,
and out of Geppetto,
who, after all, took two years to walk home
from a Siberian POW camp,
only to move back into the mud-walled ghetto
where he slept, for a while,
under his mother's bed.
And everyone knows that his mother
ran the collegiate athletic association.
She played cards and plotted every night

at a well-guarded social club.

So maybe every puppet's goal
should be to recast itself,
in the manner of the red-eyed Itsy Bitsy Spider,
newly knighted to the Round Table,
in a clearly marked box,
called to service,
along with Hedy Lamarr, the Lone Ranger, Stephen Hawking,
and the Loch Ness monster.

And in this spirit Pongo and Rico decide
to be the two halves of Odysseus
in Geppetto's little red boat,
choosing for their first companion, of many,
the ugly duckling, who now aspires to become an Eagle,

a borrowed boat being a metaphor that feels unloved,
but a boy scout being the ship of the desert.

And soon, ugly well-wishers
will crowd the dock waving.

TELLTALE SALAD DAYS

In this tale
our magical puppet heroes
land on Edible Island
with Dick the Dog
and are befriended
by Fruit and Vegetable
People,
both appetizing and kind.

The sweet, bulging ripeness
of host families
poses a new dramatic challenge
for Pongo and Rico –

While they yank the chain of
the never too intelligent Dick,
they must turn away from desire
and feel like the strangers
they are
and weak.

Why is
opening their hearts
so like
opening their stomachs?
If they were real boys
maybe desire
wouldn't leave them hollow,
feeding off the aroma of self-doubt,
hunger being so subjective.

Yet they are called upon
by the community
to foil the machinations
of King Oil and Queen Vinegar,
which they accomplish by shaming the Queen
into washing her hardwood floors
and by revealing to the King
his saturated fat content.

Temporarily relieved of
their burden,
accepting their imperfect condition
in an imperfect world,

our heroes exult:

"Convenience is not a license,"
 they shout to royalty.
"Inclination is not an invitation."
"You must know who your friends are
 and not eat them."
"It can be done, Your Majesties."

THE PRINCIPALITY OF ADENOIDS

In this first adventure past puberty,
our magical puppet heroes,
Pongo and Rico,
must save some children who are
being sacrificed to a minotaur.
And they take along as their companion
Crazy Croc.

Only it turns out children
aren't being sacrificed,
they're having their faces wiped.
And they aren't being led to a minotaur.
It's a mentor.
And Crazy Croc has changed his name.
He's Larry the Lawyer.

But then it turns out that the children are teenagers,
and they don't want their faces wiped.
And the mentor is a sports coach,
for whom winning is his only thing.

And Larry is curious about women who cross-dress as men
in lesbian bars. You can see they have no adam's apple.

And there's a giant television screen on the island
that constantly displays pictures of teenagers kissing
and buying things.
And the coach thinks he's a model for how to be strong,
but he forgets things like children's dying mothers
once the letter of intent is signed, and he encourages them
to give up their scholarships and education if they get injured,
accepting their injuries
as sacrifices on the altar of youthful idealism.

Meanwhile, Larry,
whose name is now Cowboy Bob,
has bought a motorcycle and tattoo,
and he everywhere sees images of himself as a teenager,
especially in the mirror.
Tender, excitable, unformed.
So he can't think about anybody, except himself,
or help anybody, including himself.

And Cowboy Bob is on the television screen,

along with surgically enhanced young women in bikinis
and ads for stimulating beverages
and violent boys.

And many of the teenagers start developing
multiple versions of themselves to match the many
ephemeral ideas of who they should be,
with these multiple versions sometimes hanging out together
to create nasty scenarios.

And Geppetto looks furious
but admits to nothing,
leaving Pongo and Rico
struggling to fulfill their heroic role,
thinking about the coward puppet, Peeko,
who was weak-kneed and resentful,
overreacting, confused, and sad,
and who ran away.
They suspect he was an earlier and smaller version of themselves,
made by G and considered too flawed too soon,
so that Peeko suffered not from physical fear
but from despair,
reacting to G's readiness to waste no more time

and start over.

Which prompts Pongo and Rico to focus on
the lost tribe of Peeko,
the ones who withdraw or associate,
insulated or angry, survivors or victims,
with future or no,
the ones who make themselves ugly and unpleasant,

because a cowardly puppet can sometimes escape,
even if his memories can't,
and all you need to do is to look at
the scarred runaways
sleeping in the park,
most with blankets pulled over their faces for privacy,
and see the one slender head visible,
the face of a sleeping child,

to miss the self-deprecating humor
and decency
of Crazy Croc.

SAVE THE END OF ADOLESCENCE

There are times when our magical puppet heroes,
Pongo and Rico,
must work closer to home,
like when Peeko, the cowardly puppet,
won't come out of the upstairs bathroom
where he lies on the floor
idly thumbing an erection,
playing washtub bass,
dreaming,

or spinning the toilet paper roll
for its noise, or using a stick
to push his inheritance down the
drain pipe.

And in the bath
he carefully builds himself a fort
by lining up water droplets
along the edge of the tub
with a rolled up gum wrapper.

But first taking the shaving cream
he obliterates the mirror, mirror on the wall
because of the disorienting feeling that he exists,
which, if he thought about it, is preferable to being
the weakest sissy of them all
in Geppetto's angry mirror eyes
since Geppetto made Peeko in his image,
and none of the puppets love Geppetto,
so why should he.

So it's an angry nothing who,
when Pongo and Rico appear on a ladder at the window
smiling weakly,
kicks and screams at the ducky bastard
until moldy sponge toys tumble off the wall
in an avalanche
and a glass jar falls from a shelf,
crashing in the sink near Peeko's
foamy spit.

Then guiltily,
because you wouldn't act this way if Geppetto were home,
Peeko allows Pongo and Rico to take his head,

but his head only,
down the ladder,
but not inside the house,
to Candy at the beach,
Candy with short brown hair and a sly, easy smile,
Candy who wears green shorts,
and a blue jacket against the evening air,
Candy who takes Peeko's head, is attracted to his sadness
because he's also funny, though less so now,
and kisses him lying on the sand,
eventually putting his head to her small breast.
And the puppet panics, sees himself mirrored
in his tilting, falling eyeglasses
and in the gaze of Mr. and Mrs. Raisin
on their nightly walk through the shadows.

Peeko hates himself when Candy carries him back up the ladder,
sure he won't see her again, or anyone,
but finds his torso and arms propped against the tub
shrugging
because his hips and legs have run away,
the rightest part of his body,
forcing Peeko to go after them,

a long search, in the course of which
he becomes a sympathetic friend to abandoned women
and an articulate ecologist.

And as the search goes on
Peeko's doing not bad
except for the fact he despises himself
for all the love he rejects along the way
and all the little things he's hurt,
which may be the same thing.

There's the time he flipped Sally Mander
into a trash can and closed the lid
because her jaw made clicking noises when she chewed,
paying no attention at all
to him or his information on wetlands
preservation,
an obliterated mirror,
and Peeko discovered her still in the can
the next day when he lifted the lid,
there squatting on the trash
squealing.

And the time he wanted to protect all the
Shelly Fish's in the world,
arguing on their behalf for adequate sewage treatment
and charming them,
until he abandoned their cause, feeling it hurt his image
to receive their tainted admiration.

Though Peeko starts cleaning up his act,
at the same time he makes his mark,
inoculating 1,000 walruses on ice floes,
a job that requires a surprising amount of tenderness,
and tagging them with blue spray paint
until he almost runs out of words:
Napoleon, Evita,
Lucy, Ricky,
La-Z-Boy, Credenza,
Schick, Shinola,
Peek, Eek, Echo, Pee,
Candy, and Me.

Amusing himself,
that bizarre and lonely puppet,
until it's time to go,

with feeling this time.

Finding his legs soon after
in the embrace of a
clean, jolly, and sensitive girl
who has long brown hair, arched nostrils, and a broad smile,
a girl who carries her own brand of sadness
behind her eyeglasses, eyes, and tender places.

And Peeko fits right in

causing him to reflect
that if you learn to leave with love,
maybe you can learn to stay
in the same way.

YOUNG AT HEART ISLAND

Talk about excitement,
this adventure begins with
our magical puppet heroes,
Pongo and Rico,
on a diplomatic mission
with the President of the United States,

traveling to a large-hearted archipelago
for their investiture in the Happy Guys Society,
over several fragrant evenings,
with rituals involving public bathing, long-stemmed flowers,
tall drinks of water, stacks of shellfish, wine in goblets,
musk, frog tongues, and embraceable wooden staffs,
establishing our guys as members in good standing,
Happy Guys in good standing.

Though even here Geppetto
tracks them and distracts them
by forwarding bulletins about red tide
and reporting on his health,
their nemesis, G, who

destroys their photographs,
but sends them one of himself,
imposing on them a dreary reality
like the time a gray-faced neighbor had just
separated from her husband,
broken her ring finger,
and locked herself out of her house,
and wanted the boys to climb
up a tall ladder
through a tiny, open attic window
to let her in.

But unlike the time
the boys visited an 18-year-old woman
they hadn't seen in ten years
who used to wear a dirty green hat
and now paints self-portraits in oils,
and the boys felt nervously happy to sit near her,
loving her as before,
and then to see her in a brown summer dress
through the brightly lit windows of a large house.

So when later the President,
indulging in a personal ritual,

sits in a circle of clean underwear on his penthouse floor
and has M&M candies poured on his head,
while outside the picture window
fireworks explode above a replica of
the Washington Monument,

our heroes are anything but embarrassed
by all that flag waving,
because the exploding fireworks
signify the feeling that
the ardent part of love
is real.

And the sparkling, falling embers
signify the feeling that though
Pongo and Rico are puppets,
they know what they like,
a happy place,
when they can find one,
and the final, warm, tearful presentation
of coconuts from the big island.

It could happen to you.

SPIRITUAL RETREAT ON SUNUFFA BEACH

The Curly Hair Monster
falls to earth behind them
with a soft bounce,
and our magical puppet heroes,
Pongo and Rico,
continue the dash to their boat,
no backward glances,
barely able to catch a breath,
their companion, Dick the Dog,
already aboard, barking, hair up.
The lines are slipped,
the sails fill,
another close shave.

A pair of scissors
flips through the air overhead
and lands in the bay.

But where are the men
they came with?

The whole team is missing. They
might be in the bars.
Pongo and Rico can't escape just yet.
They must explore the other end
of the island,
carefully,

where an old statue of Elvis
stands in the harbor
half covered by water,
hit by angry waves,
a bird on his head,
before a large temple,
tiled and cavernous and dirty inside,
a bus station of a temple,
with a "Please Remove Your Shoes" sign
sitting by the skate rental

and a tin duck, the size of a man,
pedaling a tricycle slowly across the floor.

No priests,
though several Red Chinese rush from an alcove

to hit the duck on the side of the head with sticks.
And a concerned Pongo and Rico
approach the duck to ask,
"How are you doing?"
"Oh, OK," says a voice from within.
And they all roll outside
to the ball field,

to a frenzy,
encouraged by prominent conservatives,
the majority whips of both houses,
naked on a platform, except for white blouses,
next to the brightly lit scoreboard
that announces
we're ahead,
while members of the team, wearing
tear-away jerseys,
dance in circles, carrying spears,
and members of the members,
dancing in smaller circles, carry smaller spears,
observed by Coach Ecstasy and the flinty Program Manager
who hug the benchwarmers,
moving from lap to lap,

until they all climb to the temple roof
and tie themselves to a May Pole,

though their rage soon causes them to
lurch off the roof edge, still tied to the May Pole,
and leaves them hanging in the air,
thrashing.

At which point,
Pongo and Rico call for reinforcements,
the American menshen,
in a thousand homemade landing craft
that fill the harbor, forcing their way through the water
and onto the beach.
There's Albert Einstein, hair flowing,
Abraham Lincoln in a 49ers cap,
Harriett the Judge's brother,
Danny and a bunch of Jewish guys,
somebody's son,

people who take care of weaker people,
though their insignia is a softball glove,
which symbolizes "My wife thinks I'm nuts."

And an excited male voice from inside a duck says,
"I'd rather be trapped in something else,
a pink mushroom maybe, riding a bigger bike."

And the quick response,
hair flowing,
"We can draw you up some plans, Mr. Crumb."

AGING ALL OVER ON CHEESE ISLAND

As Pongo and Rico,
our magical puppet heroes,
hoist their sails at the end of this adventure,
five hot-air balloons are ascending,
red, green, pink, yellow, striped,
with painted ribbons,

though from a distance
the colors are washed out
by a yellow, grainy, wavering
sky,

with seven zombie passengers per balloon,
as recommended by Jack
the Snake Boy,

while those left behind,
people,
large, round, barely mobile chefs,
300 pounds each,

in white pants, jackets, scarves, and hats,
mixing bowls, sparse beards,

cluster on the beach,
looking up,
fluttering occasionally,
like a pod of beached whales,
feeling shock
and a sudden change of heart,

empty now, after the rage
that burned them up, pointlessly,
like short-circuited wires.

The chefs recollecting that,
yes, the zombies made a lot of crumbs
when they ate and
paid no attention to the kitchen staff
lined up around them,
but wasn't it true that zombie
foot odor
had turned out to be a misplaced
bowl of balsamic vinaigrette.

And weren't the zombies making efforts
to ingratiate themselves
when they wore green felt hats,
in the manner of Robin Hood,
to the restaurant opening,
the price tags cleverly trimmed
in feather shapes.

And, face it,
weren't the zombies right,
the rémoulade did
suck.

And suddenly the chefs remembered
the night of the leaving dads,
disapproval of their culinary careers,
their emotional life
a turkey baster filled with hatred and regret.

They coldly remembered the slender teenage clerk
whose blouse fell open
when she bent forward
to fill out the dry cleaning receipt.

They coldly remembered the architect
who designed a Great Plains
boys and girls club,
two stories tall, lonely, and luminescent.

They remembered Doreen.

Then the chefs, who normally were
sealed bags of tears,
cried
because they missed their brown puppies,
gone in two hot-air balloons,
black and blue.

While Pongo and Rico, heeling to the wind,
also felt sad.
They had done the best they could
to save the rémoulade.

And the zombies,
ascending ever higher,
recalled their own surprise and anger
at the chefs' public indictments
and appeals to Harriett the Judge.

After all,
zombies paid their bills,
cared for the old and sick,
and were more proud in the face of
disrespect.
Why should they leave?
As if they counted less.

But, yes, at the time
they thought about zombie children
playing in the surf, the sun off the water,
then playing in dangerous surf.
Zombie children on bicycles.
They thought about Doreen,
who liked to touch and be touched,
the freckles on her back.
She cried at movies.

And so the zombies had decided
to place hope in a fresh start.
Five balloons, you say.
They even laughed over coffee,
sly references to turkey basters,

the usual degree of affection
and misunderstanding.
The zombies would miss the chefs, too,
a matter of zombie self-respect.

And thinking,
it's amazing how embarrassed we feel
when we're injured.

DISILLUSIONMENT IN A BRILLIANT BOWL

Pongo and Rico,
our magical puppet heroes,
must wait for Wallace,
this adventure's companion,
because the first heavy snowfall
of the year
has blanketed Hartford,
where Wallace Stevens,
not the poet,
is in bed with Becky.

The snow covers the house and yard,
muffling sound,
burying the neighbors,
this Wonderland,
as the comforter falls across Wallace's back
and settles around the couple.
The sheets are still a little cool and dry.
Like Becky's feet on Wallace's chest.
Wallace and Becky move slowly

and feel each other deeply.
Their feelings are fresh.

Later they will chase each other
around the room,
grabbing, biting, barking,
like happy huskies
in an unmarked white field.

But contrast this delight
with Pongo and Rico
and Wallace's
mission, to another cold place,
to save the children on Carnation Island
who are made of pumpkin, cheap clocks, and broken china,
dark and mushy,
noisy and inaccurate,
brittle and seemingly irreparable.
These children are 5 or 50 years old,
gray, impotent, and awkward.

They live in basements.

They are misunderstood.
Everyone thinks they are
gray, impotent, and awkward.

They seek out powerful people
to fight against in losing battles,
but they wish to hold
the powerful people's genitals.

They are jealous of their friends,
and feel they have no friends.

Their judgments are severe and moral,
stupid rationalizations
of murderous rage.

These are the children
who always feel they've failed,
poor kids,
who could climb the creaking, sagging basement stairs,
the railing wiggling on its screws,
their fingers running along the rough plaster walls,
then see light under the door at the top of the stairs,

and suddenly find themselves in a deeper basement,
darker, with less room, cobwebs in their hair,
poor kids.

And Pongo and Rico,
understanding the children's helplessness,
are reminded of family dinners long ago,
20 quiet puppets atop a red Formica table
while Geppetto stares at them hatefully,
until the puppets gag on their bananas.
Though things weren't as bad as they seemed because
Geppetto, who had a cruel older sister,
suffered too
and never died from autoerotic asphyxiation
while sucking on an orange,

and in this positive frame of mind,
Pongo and Rico and Wallace
arrive at their destination,
lead the pumpkin children out of the basements
to a park in a snowy ravine,
with instructions:

You have to do something,
like build a snowman,
go sledding,
throw snowballs but only at trees.

And later send them home, to have hot chocolate,
to watch snow flurry
around the street lights,
to crawl into bed in a prepubescent mood,
open a compartment in the belly,
adjusting the dials to wake up
at a precise time and be
ready to go bowling,
which works nearly every time,
at this time.

And where is the beauty in perfection?

THE NORTH POLE IS A BLUE CIGAR

Pongo and Rico,
our magical puppet heroes,
are soon recalled to Carnation Island,
at Christmas,
to help the children
who are made of pumpkins, cheap clocks, and broken china
because, as reported by Geppetto,
something smelled bad,
alarms ringing
with a dry sound,
the head coming off the cow creamer
when a person barely touched it.

Though pink-cheeked pumpkin children
were sledding down hillsides, yelling,
tumbling in the snow,
sweat and mist soaking their hair
and running into their eyes,
wind in their eyes,
laughing.

Still,
it was clearly a time of betrayal.
Santa and the Easter Bunny were
both taking money from toy and candy manufacturers
then poisoning the air with mutual accusations,
with predictable results
around a million Christmas trees.
The Ken doll never got
a quality gun.
On Barbie's pink convertible
the wheels were frozen.
A crouching Indian
fisted the single feather
in his lap. The soft doll
had two fingers
in a pie.
One hundred cowboys aimed crooked rifles
at plastic farm animals, a hail of fire
from atop an electric train.

During a surprise phone call
the tooth fairy made predictions
about the park when the snow melted,

new discoveries under every pillow,
not just condoms and empty beer bottles.
Panties near the trail
and a menstrual pad nearby.
Pornographic photographs
of different girls,
bored, frightened, stiff, and cynical, a few with sweet smiles.
Already
vandals threw road signs off a bridge
that landed upright beside the trail.
One hour parking.
Stop.

Clatter on the roof.
Rudolph seemed more like a faun
than a fawn. There were tally sheets,
as if masturbation were a bad thing.
The time had clearly come
to steal Santa's red suit.
The pumpkin children needed
to be loved.
Pongo and Rico failed them once,
without realizing,

by going away on business.
Not like Geppetto, though,
who expressed no remorse about
the cow creamer thing.

But if something happened in a different country,
it could happen here.
There was a long school vacation.
Guests came to dinner, women who smiled
when they thought about their first loves,
and carefully saved among old papers
photos of shy boys.
Wallace Stevens (not the poet), who brought wine,
never betrayed anyone to be with Becky,
enjoyed sex when it occurred, as suggested by the
private looks and jokes they shared,
and their relationship was textured too,
quite imperfect.

And through it all the children
enjoyed sleepovers and cocoa,
played with older toys than you might expect –
dusty dollhouses and tattered board games –

built models,
cleaned their rooms, got silly, ran around,
wrote thank you letters,
careful about their cursive,
full of love,

and then running at Pongo and Rico,
who had only been gone two hours,
to give them hugs,
almost knocking them down.

It's not the sort of thing
you plan.

FIRE IN THE BLOWHOLE

In this adventure
Pongo and Rico,
our magical puppet heroes,
sail in the tricky waters off Cape Cod,
through the frightening chop of Buzzards Bay,
and at night they sleep on rolling sand dunes
surrounded by tufts of knife-like grasses,
the ocean still churning in their heads,
imagining that buried around them
are plastic containers blackened with oil, empty beer
bottles, and tangled balls of nylon filament.
They travel with this adventure's companion,
I. P. Freely
the Handsome Sailor,
who once created a water hazard
at the miniature golf course
in Hyannis.

I. P. honed his skills at the sailing camp on Gay Bay,
their current destination,
near Barnstable, campers ages 10–14,

where his jiggling took the wind
out of everyone's sails, so they
set the boy alone on shore
with a piece of rope,
until he learned to tie knots,
and no one there to check his work.

In time our heroes anchor at Gay Bay
and walk up to tiny, rough-hewn cabins
scattered on a wooded bluff,
find narrow bunk beds, and next to every bunk
a splintery wooden hidey-hole stuffed with clothing,
where each sock and pair of underpants has a name.
The flimsy cabin doors,
on rusty, knotted, impatient springs,
are constantly slamming.

A separate building is the head,
leaking and moldy,
with pine needles washing across the floor.
This is the bathroom where
young Freely used to urinate in the shower,
though he never admitted it.
Here, in spite of the unstoppable yellow stream,

he innocently turned to face
every accuser.

Pongo and Rico and Freely have arrived,
ready to accompany senior campers and staff
on an outing. But the outing turns out to be
not what they expected.

They watch uncomfortably as
a group of prominent conservative
congressmen,
overweight and sweaty in dark suits,
crawl over the young sailors in their cramped bunks,
during quiet time,
having their pictures taken
in serious discussion
because a counselor did something nasty
to the Tunafish boy
the week before.
The campers felt ashamed.

So several campers turned away
from the congressmen,
who had salamanders on their trousers

and on their damp breast pockets,
the campers choosing instead to face the walls.
One stared at a page from Melville
that he'd tacked up to block a draft,
the edges of the paper now fluttering stiffly
like a flag in a small gale.
A congressman near this boy
remembered his own camping days,
when he inhaled and coughed as he checked out
Billy's buds. He recalled the morning after a sneak-out
when he rejected, for selfishness, ironically,
the friendship of a thin, blond friend
who had a ten-speed at home.

Bobby Tunafish was gone,
leaving behind an incomplete model
of a man-o'-war under his bunk. Over
several weeks he'd lost a lot of the pieces.

Another camper turned away from the congressmen
and looked at a photo of his father
as a young man in uniform. Watching the boy,
a prominent Jewish conservative remembered his own
camping days, when he went to Sunday Service

behind the dining hall, trying to be a good
Mr. Christian.
This congressman now fantasized about
the blond policewoman named Pepper Spray,
imagining her naked, knee-deep in the bay,
shucking and eating oysters,
against the wishes of his father.
He blamed himself for his failed marriages.

And Pongo, Rico, and I. P. Freely will soon be gone,
to save Geppetto, who is complaining
about having to build a fire
in the damp belly of a whale. It would be
just their luck if he got himself stuck at the hips
trying to crawl out the blowhole.

And another camper turned away
from the congressmen, looking instead
at some diaphanous curtains he'd hung himself,
the fabric blowing back and forth, in bright sunlight.
This was a resourceful child
who named himself Vincenzo, better than Vinnie,
and compulsively swept the cabin between activities,
and he swept the dirt path in front of the cabin door,

especially after the counselor was arrested,
when the authorities accused V of being a victim, too.
In private he kissed and stroked the door frame.

This boy worked hard on his secrets,
with a face as expressive as oatmeal. Maybe he was
a homosexual teenager with Tourette's syndrome;
he could certainly use that affliction to advantage
when it came time to yell at his mother.

So Vincenzo looked at his curtains and dreamed.
With prominent conservatives all around him
who were quietly
imagining Long Dong Silver,
he dreamed that Gary Cooper,
in the role of successful marine architect,
would walk naked out of the surf,
wearing a necklace of bubble-gum marlin spikes.
Coop would assure him that
confection is good for the soul,
and carry Vincenzo far away from this
Pleasure Island,

and we'll all feel gay.

MRS. WONG AND THE WALRUS AND THE CARPENTER

Pongo and Rico,
our magical puppet heroes,
were waiting to pay their respects
to Mrs. Wong,
who was alone on the second floor
sitting on the white plastic potty next to her bed,
her pink shift, with the brown stripes,
pulled up around her waist.
Then her potty started to float down the hallway
over the stiff old gray carpeting.
The unexpected beginning of this adventure.

A breeze from somewhere blew in Mrs. Wong's face
and made her eyes tear slightly. It ruffled her short hair,
stiff, old, and gray.
And Mrs. Wong rallied,
she'd always wanted to ride a horse,
and this was a spirited
potty.

Hawaiian music played too. It
nearly blocked out the tinny talk
of a small AM radio in Mrs. Wong's lap.

The potty spun around
and galloped down the curving staircase,
the plastic air hose still in place under Mrs. Wong's nostrils,
with fifty feet of tubing now wound around her body,
and the hose end, detached from the oxygen tank,
riding in the air behind.

The potty carried Mrs. Wong down to the basement,
where Pongo had just caught Rico cheating at croquet
by nudging his ball with a foot
to put it more in line with the wicket.
He'd been doing it all morning,
contemptuously,
and was embarrassed to be found out.

Then the rushing potty dove down a rabbit hole
that no one had noticed
between the dryer and a crumbling basement wall,
and Pongo and Rico tried to jump in after,

irritatedly pushing each other out of the way,
getting stuck, jammed together in the entrance,
a slap fight,
then falling,

to discover that the rabbit hole had green walls,
old, chipped, and soiled,
lined with brown family photographs, brown bureaus
covered with prescription bottles,
and brown nuts, young and corrosive,
like the nuts growing in Mrs. Wong's body.
Rico grabbed Pongo to make a point,
and they ended up kicking each other for a while.

It was a long fall, and Mrs. Wong called her daughter
who walked out of the rabbit hole's wall,
crying.
Mrs. Wong asked for something to eat,
they discussed mashed potatoes,
and Mrs. Wong's daughter walked back
through the wall,
some tissues balled up tightly in her hand.

Soon after,
Mrs. Wong's potty landed gently
at the bottom of the rabbit hole where
Dr. Herman Person offered her a toxic
tea cake and was impatient with her refusal.
They were in a mirrored hallway
inhabited by hatters and hares in leather chairs,
on IVs.

Pongo and Rico landed harder.
They ate the cakes they found,
after taking a long time to divide them up equally
and crumbling several.
The cakes made them swell and shrink
like the sexual organs of a smarmy parson,
a smiling man in loose pants
gently rocking in a canoe alone.

And when the action stopped,
Pongo and Rico found themselves in line at Immigration,
a single-story building with glass walls,
the boys looking out at an English garden on the other side,
feeling nervous that the immigration officer

would misconstrue their need for allergy medications.
They had no desire to wear fuzzy, fuzzy, pale blue sweaters.
They felt they deserved to pay him
each a nickel.
They stepped aside, making room for him
in the video arcade.

Meanwhile, Mrs. Wong hovered nearby,
beyond anyone's jurisdiction.
Her daughter entered through a door,
bringing lunch on a tray,
and was sent back for a napkin.
Mrs. Wong called her husband,
who walked forward from the end of the line.
She asked him about the schedule of medications
and challenged his record keeping.

Then the immigration officer confronted Pongo and Rico,
and ripped open the pillows they used
to attack each other at bedtime. He seemed to know
that they'd forgotten their times-tables
over the summer. He made them climb

into large, clear plastic hamster balls
which P & R drove into one another
until they tired.

And before anyone was ready, or when they were ready,
Mrs. Wong floated past the glass doors
to settle in the garden on the warm grass,
curled up peacefully, a pillow between her legs,
and her daughter came and bathed her.
Later, Mrs. Wong slept. No air hose.
Her hair was long now and spread out around her.

There Pongo and Rico could see Mrs. Wong,
but they weren't free to follow.
They treaded water before the desk
of a large official cockroach,
who criticized them individually
as completely as he could,
smashing things as he talked,
hurting his hand.
Surprising them by wanting their
forgiveness.

He asked, "Where is the cockroach who used to
paint in oils and develop his own photos?
Gone on the bottom
of a shoe?"

He said that all cockroach children
are born to be loved unstintingly.
He said that we are those
children, too.

"We once were all smiling young bugs," he said,
"using the drain pipes as our water slide."

Then a wave opened the glass doors,
and Pongo and Rico floated to a tea party
after Mrs. Wong.
Spring tide.

MAN / WOMAN / BIRTH / DEATH / INFINITY / THE BEAV

In this adventure
Pongo and Rico,
our magical puppet heroes,
have gone as far as they can go,
to Sugar Pops Island where life originated,
floating in a bowl,
at the edge of the world on Saturday morning,
in an empty house with grease spatters on the stovetop,
toast crumbs on the floor with butter, and brown goo in the bottom trays
of the humming refrigerator,
the whole making some kind of chemical reaction.

In the beginning
a milky rain named Ward
blew through the open kitchen window,
wetting the curtains, splashing down on the sturdy plastic dishes
piled high in the sink,
and June grew up between a couple of jelly glasses
to clean up the mess,
naked and unashamed,
both fathered by Ward and impregnated by him.

She soon gave birth to Ward the man
on the living room couch, where they drank coffee
after dinner, uncomfortable over
their strange intimacy,
for Ward and June were father and mother
to each other,
son and daughter,
husband and wife.

Nothing much was on television at the time,
just game shows.

Later they felt better,
when Ed Sullivan came on,
as June dished them out a couple of bowls
of Neapolitan ice cream.
No one had ever loved them before,
certainly not the top-hatted tycoon
who held both the mortgage on their house
and the majority interest in the network,
the same guy who red-lined Amos and Andy's neighborhood
and scripted a ballooning military budget.

Then Ward and June got on with the business of
creating Eden.
They had plants for hair — scrub in Ward's ears,
marshes under his arms, thickets in his nose,
the waving grasses on June's pudenda,
a few vines hanging from around her nipples.
So that as Ward and June scratched themselves,
or stretched, or shuffled from couch to kitchen,
seeds and cuttings fell to earth
along with animals that tumbled from the forests, jungles, and seabeds,
and ran away.

June kept up the effort, watered the geranium seeds
until they bloomed and died,
fed the cocker spaniel until it grew fat
and gassy.
Ward over-fertilized the lawn that always turned brown.
He donated animals to collections around the world.

Later, a teenager named Wallace was born
who worried a lot about the small number of girls in Paradise.
Wally would lose himself in the bathroom,
looking at his growing knuckles and pimples, masturbating.

And a pubescent boy named Theodore was born,
sensitive, insecure, nicknamed "Beaver" or "the Beav,"
who drank beer behind the high school and shoplifted full of fury
from the Woolworth's downtown.

It seemed that the family's relationships soured as the boys' attention
turned away from wholesome entertainment
that starred their parents.
The family's difficulties worsened along with Ward's
business and colitis problems.

Ward's future in nuclear power was undermined when
General Electric hung June's brother and sister
for giving away its secrets to the Democratic Party.
Here Ward had pioneered the use of atomic energy to create
Coca-Cola, Gravy Train, and individually wrapped slices of cheese,
and he still generated frequent atomic blasts
in his basement workshop called Hades,
but was burdened with a mushroom cloud of debt.

In these troubled days
Ward would despair of getting his head above
the radioactive wastewater,

then charge upstairs from Hades full of fury
to ask why Wally and the Beav hadn't volunteered
to pump out the septic tank for love.
He pounded on the bathroom door,
but usually couldn't find the Beav.

And if he saw Wally and the Beav lying on the couch,
each with a head on June's lap, being petted,
Ward would walk into the room without a word
and turn off the TV.
Always the alarm on his watch would go off
because something was cooking downstairs.

Happiness was rare, occurring only late at night,
when Ward sat all alone in a darkened room
watching Buddy Hackett on The Tonight Show.
From the next room Wally resented
the sudden bursts of laughter.

So it was into this environment that Pongo and Rico landed,
like prodigal sons or naive critics,
to be greeted by a castrato named Milton Berle,
not the famous cross-dresser but an agent of the tycoon,

who assured them that June was always cute,
Ward was always right,
and thirty years would pass in as many days,
as if that were a good thing.

Uncle Miltie showed them his copy of the good book
by Arbitron, whose large-print edition was used
to hold people in front of the local news
with pressure on their tender parts
because self-sacrifice was required in the
fight against communism.

And as an object lesson
he pointed out the useless remains
of Howdy Doody, tangled in his strings and rolling in the tide,
who had exploded from anger because he
never got any respect. Though the explosion exposed a tender core,
Howdy was ever the outsider,
unconcerned with who had the bomb.

So that P & R knew they had to leave
like Tonto to The Little Big Horn

or Jimmy Olsen from The Daily Planet
after Superman's suicide,
to find the big On/Off on the other side of the island,
the switch that would expose all of the dirty secrets and lies,
a mechanical Walter Cronkite.

Though in a cowardly act, Pongo and Rico
sailed quickly past June's eyes that shone like Merrie Melodies,
even as she waded out to them excitedly,
dog heads and snakes hanging off of her,
fish falling from her armpits,
and they wrote a bad review of her loving performance,
while Ward felt the hurt from the front yard,

P & R having failed to realize
that you can talk to the TV all you want without effect
except for the pain you cause your family.

AT THE MALL OF THE LARGE INTESTINE: "ATTENTION SHOPPERS!"

Having sailed to the end of the world
our magical puppet heroes, Pongo and Rico,
negotiate their way around the surgically-enhanced promontories
of June Cleaver
and past the hellfire of Ward's basement workshop,
surprised to find that these two depressives are Adam and Eve
and that their legacy includes the Action News team of Abel
and Lori Nakagawa at 6:00 and 11:00, yellow police tape,
Cain's summary of sports scores and highlights
from around the league, Chopper 7
eye-in-the-sky, and
an isobar-savvy, well-intentioned snake named Sir Percy
nervously trying to ingratiate himself
in spite of the five-day forecast.

All of which determines Pongo and Rico
to make the big On/Off their grail,
converting odyssey to quest, a seeming inevitability now,
though no more anticipated than any other part
of their windblown journey.

They adopt the weatherman as this adventure's companion
when he frees himself from June's Medusa-like coif and,
breasting the icy water,
catches P & R's little red boat to wiggle aboard,
with no ill effects on the crew
save for chronic problems with tight shoulders
and stiff necks.

It is Sir Percy who guides our heroes to an obscure cove
to behold a giant puppet head on a high, grassy bluff,
open-mouthed and shining-eyed, staring out to sea
past the ocean waves that hit the edge of the earth's bowl
and slop over.

And in a beach cave directly below the puppet head,
our heroes find and enter a giant pair of puppet feet,
round and metallic and brightly lit inside
like two gutted submarines,
with a few bare metal bunks and a small stack of weather maps
worn thin and torn from erasures, that Percy attempts to clarify,
plus boxes of souvenirs from P & R's own travels,
including the pubic hair monster's spring molt,
an open vat of balsamic vinaigrette,

little plastic pumpkins overflowing with hard candy,
a striped blue-and-white sailor blouse,
and an oil painting of a walrus
named Capacious.
There are letters, too, all addressed to men,
"Let's talk again, soon. OK?"
And one of Geppetto's diapers
and odd splats on the ceiling
and a framed law degree
and a picture of Saint Sebastian
and a pile of wet rugs

and a coupon for a free popcorn, hot dog, and large Coke
at the Gluteus Cineplex
for their next ordeal,
the premiere of the new fall lineup of must-see entertainment.
So they climb a ladder past a quaking knee,
their masculinity trembling,
P & R reminded of the time they were poised to jump off a shaken rung
onto Geppetto's angry neck,
and thinking still that they
are owed a break.
Finally settling into red plush seats,

their laps filled with refreshments
beside the curtained butt hole.

Then a TV exec, her long red fingernails flashing,
rides on stage atop a large, voluptuous woman on all fours,
the underling's breasts bulging at the neck of her loose cotton shirt,
and the executive dismounting to explain the anticipated demographics of
"World's Funniest Police Beatings,"
"My Three Dead Sons,"
"Rapist Knows Best," and
"My Mother the Whore,"
and to clarify the parental-discretion advisory
that introduces Saturday morning's commercials
in which little darlings try to rip mommy's breasts off
for giving them the kind of breakfast cereal they hate
and enlist a toy army
to gang rape and torture baby brother,
then eat mommy for lunch with cinnamon on top
and push daddy in the dirty diaper bag
and roll him around for a while,
the babies finally transforming themselves
into Tinker Bells and bluebirds and wounded royalty,
happily ever after,

the network presentation interspersed with unremembered home movies of
baby Pongo and baby Rico, as manipulated by Geppetto
on thick, black strings,
in a flailing dance and singing,
"Love, love, love,
love, love, love.
Everything is fine."
With frequent taped applause and wild laughter.

And when it's over
Pongo and Rico and Percy,
feeling changed, perhaps,
like the shy but grateful recipients of a rectal makeover
on Jerry Springer,
are understandably ready
to escape to the Genital Playground across the street
to an operational giant crane
with four reverse gears and one forward,
but how many do you need,
an extensive set of shift levers and controls across the dash,
with many girders and panels lying about for creative play,
and a telescoping crane arm that reaches out of sight
like a kite, so relaxing.

And they'd never give up their turns,
in spite of the leaking lunch boxes behind the seat
and the insect infestation,
even if Geppetto showed up again to burn their feet with a hot spoon
or unleash his swarming minions of little dagger men.
Enjoying themselves for once, our heroes are confident
that all of their permits are in order, and feel sure that
a good mother would insist they go out and play
after all that TV.

And, in fact, they are indulged in their efforts at heavy construction
by a community of sympathetic travel agents
in beachwear of many colors,
zaftig veterans of nuclear war
and heavy menstrual flow,
who slide over to our guys in the sand box
and with bright eyes compliment their larger purpose,
softly encouraging them
to sightsee, nose around, expose themselves,
take in the world,
move about the cabin,

to eventually climb the next ladder of their journey and

taste the flavors
of foodstuffs fresh and spoiled, complicated recipes,
spices, stores of refrigerated desserts
that must be consumed before their expiry date,
Percy's favorite apples,
and several sacraments,

but, before they go,
to finish this leg of their travels
with local festivals and exploding fireworks
never mentioned in Fodor's, Rough Guide, or Lonely Planet,
a happy reminder of the old saw
to always take a trip yourself
if you want it done right,

which includes a tour of nothing good
in season.

MEAT TENDERIZER, ANOTHER CONDIMENT

You may remember how the odyssey began
with the Ugly Duckling shifting its damp bottom uncomfortably
during a community meeting
as Geppetto explained that he wanted a different birdie
to lay the puppet company's
golden eggs.

And Pongo and Rico, our magical puppet heroes,
who felt pigeonholed along with their ugly friends,
could no longer accept Geppetto's line that
there were no small parts
when they had small parts.

So P & R set off in their little red boat,
went searching for the big On/Off, their quest,
being tired of the same old crap on TV year after year,
to explore the sacred interior of a giant puppet statue,
from feet to ass to genitals to stomach and points north,
wondering now if their journey would end with their latest discovery,
a ratty, red, meat-like Muppet tightly bound with duct tape,

a Muppet clutching within its fetters
the tabernacle at the statue's heart.

Though here Pongo and Rico hesitated, unsure about making a rescue,
because they recognized the red Muppet
as the set designer from the puppet theater, an incompetent
who was always trapping them behind jammed doors,
against freshly painted backdrops,
in corners of his collapsing sets with newly waxed floors,
and causing them to miss their entrances, flub their cues,
fall on their faces,
fail to get the girl, be the perpetual outsiders,
much to the director's sneering amusement.

They hesitated, expecting the worst
from this unhelpful brother,
until an elderly stranger selling New Balance sneakers,
Chiron the Centaur,
a horse's ass with a large brain
and an outsize collection of dangly objects,
walked out of the shadows and argued convincingly
that they had to trust somebody
some time.

The newly shod Pongo and Rico
unwound the heart Muppet and relieved it of its burden
while Chiron looked on impassively.

Then P & R carefully lowered the tabernacle to the floor,
lifted the lid slightly, and were horrified
because out flew all the evil hatchlings of the heart,
including a betrayed salamander, a xenophobic debutante,
a cantor who sang shvartzer songs badly,
pimps, astrologers,
conservative congressmen in special session, editors,
too many evils to count,
and Pongo and Rico chewed their arms
till they got splinters in their mouths,
and at the bottom of the ark lay the dusty scripts
of Geppetto's Bible stories,
some home truths from the distant past.

And then looking for a way to undo their actions,
to enlist the aid of all the king's horses and men,
Pongo and Rico analyzed every manuscript page,
starting with Geppetto's story of Genesis,
in which God circumcised Adam on the sixth day

and then did it again on the seventh,
reading that God was also disappointed in Adam's pointy head
so He went to the med school library to read up.
How God asked Adam and Eve to name the beasts
and hated every suggestion.
How God was furious and expelled Adam and Eve from the Garden
for eating fruit from the tree of knowledge when
they could have chosen a less expensive item off the menu,
like Salisbury steak.

But next, reading further,
Pongo and Rico found supplements to the scriptures,
forgotten stories that were in their own handwriting,
such as how Cain first tried to slay Abel
by pushing him off the ironing board
during a kiddy photo session in their living room.

Geppetto wrote that God asked Noah to make an ark,
found fault with Noah's work, and finished the job Himself.
God was irritated when He later realized that Noah
had gone inside dejectedly
and turned on TV.

P & R's story, which followed Geppetto's, described how Noah
couldn't navigate the ark at all
after listening in the stalls
to the braying of angry congressmen
from both parties.

Geppetto wrote that God didn't like the people in Sodom and Gomorrah
because they talked about things and had sex. That God
was especially angry at the Gomorrites who were money-grubbing doctors,
Irish politicians, Axis officers, and Jews who wore sideburns in the Sixties,
so He dropped the bomb.

Pongo and Rico wrote how
Lot was afraid to love his wife after the incident,
and the consequences for them both.

And one of Geppetto's stories said that God railed at Job's complacency
following his acceptance to an Ivy League college out of town,
and that's why God put the young man's ancient beagle to sleep
during prom season, plus His allergies,
and never said a word.

P & R's script said something about how Job wore a blue tux

and farted loudly at the reception. And so on.

And after reading all this with care,
it was evident to Pongo and Rico
that they could never contain the evil,
the feelings of shame and guilt,
especially considering the contributions to this gospel
they had personally laid down.
It was obvious to the puppets that no exegesis
could fill the tabernacle's void.

So Chiron led our heroes away from the heart
and sent them up a ladder to the eyes of the giant puppet statue,
an aerie that looked out on the ocean
and the edge of the world,
where P & R found
that the wind and waves had risen in the small bay
near the statue's feet,
that the surf was now roaring around the bay's perimeter
and tearing at the narrow beach.

Below them Pongo and Rico saw a group of divorced men
working energetically,

driving classic cars onto the sand
and raising high-flying systems of cables and screens
to keep the surf from destroying everything.
The men were mostly separated from their children.

Also on the beach
was a young woman with red lines of emotion on her cheeks.
She had dark hair and dark eyeglasses, a lithe body
that was a little wide at the hip, and a smile like a sunbreak.
She wrapped her arms around one man's waist, and her eyes
explored his face expectantly
as she explained to him with quiet words that she would love him,
and the man was trying to love her back,

which Pongo and Rico from their perch,
the wind stinging their faces,
finally recognized as their manly dilemma
and regret.

CIAO, UGLY

In what appears to be their final adventure,
Pongo and Rico, the magical puppets,
have been imprisoned in the brain of a giant puppet statue,
doing hard time
on a small island at the end of the earth,
because their inability to love
is eroding beaches, expensive white sand beaches,
and infecting innocent brown-skinned locals,

though, ironically, P & R had traveled this far
for the purpose of writing new parts for themselves,
improved heroes' parts,
in which they are competent saviors as well as
brave venturers into the unknown. Yes,
they had called themselves hopeful heroes
all along.

Only, having gone as far as they could go and landing here,
Pongo and Rico found a statue with a Muppet heart,
and the heart was crammed with Geppetto's old scripts

that cast Pongo as Snow White, stalked by the seven little dagger men,
that cast Rico as a mattress stain
in *The Princess and the Pea*,

which seemed equivalent to a life sentence
and reminded P & R of the only time they'd cried,
when Geppetto denied them tough-guy roles
in the puppet *Treasure of the Sierra Madre*,
with the message that life wouldn't supply
a stinking thing they wanted.

Though Geppetto had the nerve to cry for them once,
when P & R found a pair of pants
and something to put in them
for their brother Peeko
on their only visit home.
G cried because he wanted Pongo and Rico
to want to never leave.
It was surprising because normally
Geppetto never told them anything straight,
only through his scripts,
which were distributed by a longtime assistant.

Had Geppetto scripted their inability to love?
He surely hadn't scripted all the ways they felt,
or the awful ways they always felt,
but he had taught them the consequences
of failing to read between the lines.
So maybe that was the clue
to figuring out how a person goes bad.
Not by going where Geppetto wants you to go,
like to the puppet theater.
Not by going where Geppetto wants you not to go,
like to the end of the world.
But by going where G never tells you
to go or not to go,
to the heart of the matter,
a place where you live and never leave, your secret hideout:
Geppetto's childhood, his bedroom, and his grave.

So, looking for places marked by emptiness,
having noted that prisoners always gather in the kitchen at parties,
never sit on the new divan,
Pongo and Rico took their drinks and napkins and cheesy hors d'oeuvres
and wandered into the living room,
piled furniture to the ceiling and climbed through a trap door

to the warden's command post,
where, not being control freaks,
Pongo and Rico found and pulled
the big On/Off.

And were startled at the changes,
how suddenly the statue had to get up several times a night
to go to the bathroom,
how the statue had to avoid coffee in the P.M.
and forgo Mexican food completely.
How a ridiculous profusion of hair
sprouted from the statue's ears,
how the mechanism was free
to die in thirty years,
though the benefits of this freedom
eluded the transformed Pongo and Rico
with their new humanity.

Then they climbed up the last ladder
and poured like water from a fountain
onto the activity of a rooftop park,
into long grass that looked like dark wavy hair,
where brown-skinned children ran and laughed.

A road led directly to this playground from the beach below,
easy access, and the parking lot on a sunny day
was full of brilliant women and colors.

Ugly Duckling was there too, looking for them,
having just flown in with a message from home,
where Geppetto lay in hospital complaining.
It seems that although P & R had kept Geppetto's secrets
as long as they could, like heroes,
the old man was dying.

So they set sail for the puppet theater
on a carefully plotted course,
but different from the one that brought them here,
choosing a southern route through sad latitudes,
determined to brave strong currents, sunken hazards, freak weather,
whatever it took, to acquire emotions honestly,
when possible, and minds for mysteries,

but mostly to learn compassion,
enough to mitigate Pongo and Rico's chief quality, even now,
awkwardness.

This book was designed by Celeste Ericsson.

It is set in ITC Bookman, "a sturdy workhorse type," designed by Ed Benguiat in 1975. It was printed by Edwards Brothers Incorporated.

The illustrations were executed in watercolor and guache, and in pen and ink.